Sophia Anne Mosley

Manual of Poetical Effusions

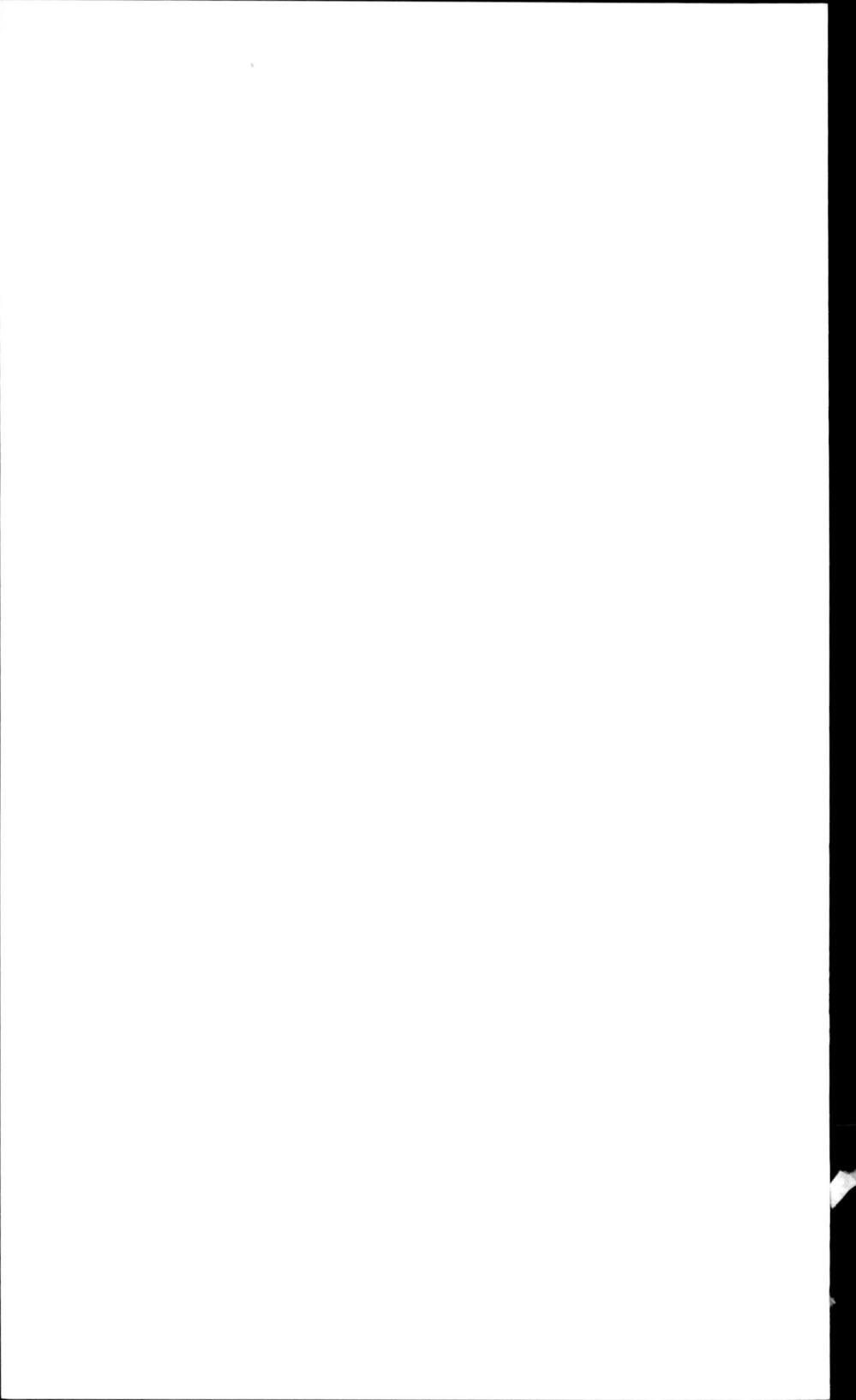

Sophia Anne Mosley

Manual of Poetical Effusions

ISBN/EAN: 9783337778088

Printed in Europe, USA, Canada, Australia, Japan

Cover: Foto ©Thomas Meinert / pixelio.de

More available books at **www.hansebooks.com**

MANUAL

OF

Poetical Effusions.

BY

SOPHIA ANNE MOSLEY.

LONDON:

PRINTED BY J. BLOCKLEY, HAWLEY TERRACE,

CAMDEN TOWN.

———

1860.

ADDRESS TO MY READERS.

To you, my Readers, I these Poems send,
With the best wishes of a Christian Friend,
And the bright hope, that sentiments express'd,
Will find an ardent response in each breast.
Consoling Verses, oft to minds impart
An influence sweet, to soothe and cheer the heart ;
Such is the wish I entertain for these—
The mind to tranquilize, the heart to ease.
When joy and happiness around us shine,
Ah! how enchanting—truly, how sublime!
To strike the Chord, attune the Poet's Lyre
To strains of rapture which such Gifts inspire.
God bless these Verses with the Heav'nly charm,
In joy to sanctify, in sorrow calm.
And now, kind Readers, with this end in view,
Accept the Poems that I offer you.

CONTENTS,

	PAGE
Address to my Readers	5
The Pleasures of Religion	9
"Casting all your Care upon God"	20
For Mercy and Forgiveness	13
For Divine Aid in Affliction	15
For God's Blessing	12
Faith in Prayer	17
Hope in God	19
"Pray without Ceasing"	39
Hymn of Gratitude	10
"Judge not"	42
"Love one Another"	44
The first and last Miracle	45

The Christian Works from Love 40

" My Peace I give unto you" 37

Invocation to the Deity 22

The Wish 35

To a Sister on her Marriage 32

Ode to Domestic Bliss 34

Ode to Faith, Hope, and Love 36

On contributing to the Bible Society...... 30

On Providence 17

On the Sacrament..................... 18

On Time.............................. 46

To the Memory of a Beloved Mother 41

To the Memory of a Dear Sister 24

To the Memory of a Lamented Brother .. 27

To the Memory of a much-lov'd Sister 23

The Christian's bright Hope of the Spirit's
        Glory 29

The Angel Spirits..................... 48

Poetical Effusions.

ON THE PLEASURES OF RELIGION.

Religion heightens ev'ry joy,
    Alleviates all our pains :
No earthly cares can long annoy,
    Where pure Religion reigns.

That lovely Peace, so calm, so pure,
    Which in the Christian glows,
Religion only can secure,
    Religion only knows.

HYMN OF GRATITUDE.

Divine Redeemer! O Thou God of Love!
  Saviour! Adored Lord, thro' whom alone
My feeble prayers ascend to Heav'n above,
  And gain admittance at thy Father's Throne—

Shine, Bounteous God, upon my inmost soul:
  My mind illumine with thy Heavenly Grace:
Direct my will, each erring thought control:
  Turn on me, Lord, the brightness of thy Face.

O! guide my steps in Heavenly Wisdom's ways,
  Where peace and pleasure are alone combined;
In active Virtue, and in pious Praise,
  May I life's true enjoyment ever find.

O! that I could more thankfully express
  The debt of gratitude I owe to Thee;
With heart, and soul, I would my Saviour bless,
  For every bounteous gift bestowed on me.

But still, alas! how cold, how hard my heart;
  How void my soul of pure and fervent love;
Yet, Lord, forgive me, and that grace impart
  Which those receive who seek it from above.

Almighty Giver of consummate joy,
    From Thee alone can solid comfort flow :
For nothing ever shall that bliss destroy,
    Which only those who trust in Thee can know.

Grant me a Heart, more gratefully inclined—
    A Soul, transported with thy Love divine—
A Will, more to thy Holy Will resigned—
    Ah! make me, Gracious Saviour, fully thine.

Give me an Angel's tongue, a Seraph's lyre,
    To praise and thank Thee for thy love to me;
Inflame my heart with pure celestial fire,
    Glowing with fervent gratitude to Thee.

O ! while I've life, may I that life employ,
    To sound the praises of my God and King;
Then, Lord, translate me to those realms of Joy,
    Where I shall ever Hallelujahs sing.

A HYMN FOR GOD'S BLESSING

Benignant Being! Gracious Power!
Who hast upheld me to this hour,
O! suffer not my steps to stray,
But lead me in thy heav'nly way.

My God, from whom all blessings flow,
Teach me thy Holy Will to know;
Grant me thy Spirit to act right,
And ever serve Thee with delight.

For all thy goodness, Lord, to me,
A thankful heart I offer Thee;
Fain would I love Thee more and more,
My Saviour bless, my God adore.

Jesus! my Rock, and gracious Friend,
On whom alone my hopes depend,
Never, ah! never let me rove—
Bless, and protect me, with thy Love.

In hard temptation's trying hour,
Do thou support me, with thy power;
In sorrow and affliction's day,
Assuage my grief, and soothe my way.

When Love and Mercy on me shine,
Then make me more than ever Thine;
Great God! assist me then to raise
My grateful heart in joyful praise.

Who can thy Mercies e're express?
So undeserved, so numberless;
And yet, tho' frail my worship be,
My fervent thanks I offer Thee.

Saviour! Thy Heavenly Grace afford:
Prosper, and guide me, Bounteous Lord:
For all thy wondrous blessings prove
That God, my God, is God of Love.

A HYMN,

ENTREATING FOR MERCY AND FORGIVENESS.

Almighty Father! God of Love!
  A contrite sinner see;
Oh! send thy Spirit from above,
  To aid and strengthen me.

Be not extreme my faults to mark ;
　My errors, pray forgive ;
For shouldst Thou ev'ry sin remark,
　Before Thee, who can live ?

But look upon my Saviour's Face,
　Who intercedes for me,
And for his all-prevailing Grace,
　Thy Mercy let me see.

Unworthy, ah ! I know I am,
　Of all thy favours past ;
E'en when I do the best I can,
　How very frail, at last.

Then grant me thy assisting aid,
　For in Thee I am strong ;
Nor leave me, for my virtues fade,
　And then, alas ! do wrong.

I'll seek Thee—O ! forsake me not ;
　I'll ask, I'll knock, I'll pray,
That Thou, whate'er may be my lot,
　Wilt bless and guide my way.

A HYMN,

IMPLORING DIVINE ASSISTANCE IN THE DAY OF AFFLICTION.

O God! who marks a sparrow's fall,
    Who even numbers ev'ry hair,
O! hear a suppliant sinner's call,
    Attend unto my fervent pray'r.

Dost Thou disdain the silent tear?
    Unheeded see, the Heav'n-rais'd eye?
And will my God refuse to hear,
    The inward, heart-felt, heaving sigh?

O no! my Saviour, ever kind
    To those who put their trust in Thee;
May I to thy will be resign'd,
    And do Thou love, and strengthen me.

By fear assail'd, by grief oppress'd,
    Ah! leave me not in deep despair;
Speak peace unto my troubled breast,
    And let me cast on Thee my care.

Why should I doubt? What can I fear,
  When I upon my God depend?
All shall be well, if Thou art near,
  My Rock! my Saviour! and my Friend!

Assur'd that Thou dost all things well,
  Even in sorrow's trying hour,
Ah! never may a thought rebel,
  Against thy wisdom, love, and power.

What Thou ordain'st I know is best,
  And tho' by me not understood,
Let me upon thy promise rest,
  That all at last shall work for good.

My Saviour, here, with tender love,
  Vouchsafe to bless and prosper me,
Then take me to the realms above,
  To dwell in Happiness with Thee.

FAITH IN PRAYER.

I will not doubt, still less despair,
Since God Almlghty answers Prayer;
I know not how, or when, or where,
Yet this I know, God answers Prayer.

The Lord, who counts each single hair,
Will not disdain to answer Prayer;
To God I'll bring each wish and care,
Assur'd my Saviour answers Prayer.

Ah! who will for a moment dare
To limit God, who answers Pray'r?
Lord, I believe, each Blessing rare
Will be the Gift that answers Prayer.

ON PROVIDENCE.

My God, I trace thy hand in all:
I own thy sovereign Love:
Assur'd that nothing can befall,
But what's ordain'd above.

Tis bliss indeed, on Earth to know,
  That God appoints my lot;
My God, who can all good bestow,
  I pray, forsake me not.

Lord, turn not Thou thy face away:
  Oh! look in mercy down;
Direct my choice, and guide my way:
  My path with blessings crown.

Then gratefully I'll raise my voice,
  Thy goodness to adore;
In God, my Saviour, I rejoice,
  And praise Thee evermore.

ON THE SACRAMENT.

Dear Saviour, 'tis thy Merits that I plead,
  Thy precious Body, thy atoning Blood;
Lord! may my soul for ever on them feed,
  And bless them to me, for Eternal good.

To this rich Feast I would with faith draw nigh:
  To this pure Fountain of Celestial Love:
Seek, from my Saviour, a bounteous supply,
  Of Pardon, Peace, and Comfort from above.

My sins, tho' scarlet, shall be white as snow :
Tho' red like crimson they shall be as wool :
For me the streams of Heav'nly Mercy flow,
My Jesus robes me, and my Cup is full.

HOPE IN GOD.

Rejoice, my Soul, dispel all fear,
For God, thy God, is ever near ;
Saviour, I seek for aid from Thee—
Oh! God, my God, remember me.

In God I hope, on Him depend,
Who is my Rock, my bounteous Friend ;
To Thee with joy I make my Pray'r,
Assur'd I never need despair.

In God I trust, on Him rely,
Who marks each anxious, heart-felt sigh ;
Prosper me, Lord of Heav'n above ;
Bless, and guard me, Almighty Love.

A HYMN.

___

Casting all your care upon God, for He careth for you."—1 Peter, v. 7.

___

Saviour! I bend before thy throne,
 Casting on Thee each anxious care:
Oh! deign to make my cause thine own,
 Vouchsafe to hear my feeble Pray'r.

My God, each erring wish efface;
 With love illumine all my soul;
Let the rich beams of heav'nly grace
 Each hope, each fond desire control.

So very weak and frail am I,
 To Thee I dare not raise my voice,
But on my Jesus I rely,
 And in His merits I rejoice.

O! listen to the Pray'r of one
 Who seeks Thee, in this hour of need;
Yet, Father, let Thy will be done:
 Speak but the word—'tis good indeed.

Each anxious thought, each heaving sigh,
  The fervent breathing of each pray'r
On Cherub's wings ascend on high,
  To meet a kind Redeemer there.

I would not ask Thee, Lord, to give,
  What Thou in wisdom would deny,
But I entreat Thee to forgive,
  Whate'er is wrong, in wish or sigh.

Prosper me, then, in all I do—
  Be Thou my guide—direct my way—
Teach me, good Lord, where'er I go,
  To serve Thee well, by night and day.

My God, if pleasing in thy sight,
  That I should thus thy goodness trace,
Grant me thy Spirit to act right:
  In time of need afford thy grace.

May I for ever grateful prove,
  For Gifts my Saviour deigns to grant;
Permit me not from Thee to rove,
  Nor aught my Saviour to supplant.

But may my lips with praise express
  The grateful feelings of my heart;
With all my power my Saviour bless,
  For ev'ry joy He does impart.

Thy grace and blessing from on high,
   Do Thou, kind God, to me extend;
So may I live, that when I die,
   My Spirit may to Thee ascend.

There, in eternal happiness,
   In sweet communion of Soul,
I would my dear Redeemer bless,
   While ages shall·on ages roll.

INVOCATION TO THE DEITY.

Almighty Maker of my Frame,
   Teach me to know how great Thou art,
And let me praise thy glorious Name,
   With joyful lips, and thankful Heart.

Teach me to mark that Sovereign Pow'r,
   Whose goodness rules the world with Love;
In ev'ry place, at every hour,
   Shine brightly on me, from above.

Ah! sanctify each Gift bestow'd—
   Impart thy Grace, that I may bless
The bounteous Hand, from which it flow'd,
   And gratefully my thanks express.

Alas! I've nothing to defray
   The debt that I've contracted here;
And yet, my God, receive, I pray,
   The incense of a Heart sincere.

This humble Tribute of my Praise
   Is all the Offering I bring;
With gratitude my voice I'll raise,
   And of God's goodness ever sing.

This favour'd Privilege I claim,
   Thro' Christ, who shed for me His blood:
The Saviour, of Eternal fame,
   The Lord God, Holy, Just, and Good.

IN MEMORY OF

A BELOVED SISTER.

Whither, dear Sister, whither hast thou fled?
Must I believe, alas! that thou art dead?
Thy sister mourns for thee, laments with tears,
The gentle playmate of her youthful years.

So young, so mild, affectionate and kind,
Belov'd the most by those who knew her mind;
O! how regretted have you been by me,
How oft I've longed that face once more to see.

And art thou now for ever from me torn?
No; I shall see again that much-lov'd form.
O! Gracious God! thy Spirit freely give,
That I may die to sin, and for Thee live.

Then, when my Sun is set, my race is run,
And the short thread of my existence spun,
O! may I meet again my Sister dear.
In the bright regions of a happier sphere.

TO THE MEMORY OF

A DEEPLY-REGRETTED SISTER.

Beloved Spirit, much-lamented Maid,
  How dear thy Image to thy Sister's mind;
Within the tomb thy mortal frame is laid,
  To earth no longer is thy Soul confin'd.

How am I wont to dwell on that sweet smile,
  Depicting plainly tenderness and love;
That gentle conduct, meek and free from guile,
  Fit for the company of Saints above.

But now no more exposed to human view
  Is that dear Form, in which each virtue shone:
Tender, compassionate, sincere and true—
  Yes! these were graces which were all thy own.

Why should I grieve the loss of her, whose fate,
  So far exceeds what mortals here enjoy?
Why weep for one who's only past the gate
  Which is the entrance to Eternal Joy?

Why should I grieve the loss of her, who's gone
  Where peace and happiness alone can dwell?
I'll cease to sorrow, weep, and mourn for one,
  Who tastes such pleasures as we can't foretell.

The gracious God, who rules the world in Love,
  Chastises and corrects us for our good:
The Saviour, who descended from above,
  Was crucified to save us, if we would.

What if He governs us with iron rod?
  Divides and severs us from those most dear?
Our Heavenly Father, and our gracious God,
  Will not forsake us; He is ever near.

c

And thou, blest soul, tho' I no more shall see,
  No more shall hold sweet converse with on
    earth,
Still that kind God, who guides and comforts me,
  Cheers and delights thee, with celestial mirth.

To my imagination ever dear,
  Tho' now no longer present to my view,
To memory, to recollection dear—
  I ne'er, fond Sister, ne'er can forget you.

To fairer Mansions has thy Spirit fled,
  To bless thy God, thy Saviour to adore :
Follow'd where Christ himself the way has led,
  Where sorrow, pain, and grief shall be no
    more.

Since the same Pow'r o'er both our Spirits reigns,
  Protects and guards us, tho' now far apart,
To that kind God, who still in mercy deigns
  To look on me, I'll give my Soul and Heart.

Teach us, good God, who yet on earth do dwell,
  To know thy righteous way, and do thy Will;
Grace grant to us, who from thy glory fell,
  Wash and forgive, and sanctify us still.

Then when our frail and fleeting course is run,
  And we on silver Wings to Heav'n shall soar,
Receiv'd by God, redeem'd by Christ His Son,
  We join our friends, and meet to part no more.

Then in eternal Bliss, and endless day,
  Our dear Redeemer's wondrous Love we'll
    sing:
No longer vested in encumb'ring clay,
  We'll praise our Saviour and adore our King.

TO THE MEMORY OF

A BELOVED BROTHER.

Another link from earth is flown,
  Another cord is broken—
Thus drawing us still nearer Home,
  Thus ripening us for Heaven.

'Tis hard to part from those we love,
  To sever every tie;
Ah! say not so, but look above,
  To realms beyond the sky.

The forms we love so much on earth
    Are only made for time;
But JESUS claims our second birth—
    The Spirit is Divine.

You'll meet again, ah! do not doubt—
    Then, mourner, grieve not thus;
The dear departed has been bought
    By CHRIST, who died for us.

Then, why lament?   He is not lost,
    He's only gone before,
To join the brilliant Heavenly Host,
    Where bliss reigns evermore.

Ah! let the eye of Faith discern
    The light that burns so dim :
For, tho' he cannot now return,
    We still may go to him.

"I love my JESUS," was his cry,
    When lingering here below;
And now, with JESUS ever nigh,
    His love shall brighter glow.

For JESUS loves him with a love
    All powerful, Divine;
And, though He reigns in Heaven above,
    Blest SAVIOUR! Thou are mine.

Ecstatic thought! And art thou mine?
  Then let me cease to grieve,
For all in CHRIST shall ever shine,
  Eternally to live.

THE CHRISTIAN'S BRIGHT HOPE
OF THE SPIRIT'S GLORY.

Christian rejoice, thy hope is great—
Reflecting on a future state;
Be comforted for those so dear,
Tho' they no longer sojourn here.

When flown from Earth, how sweet to trace
Their Spirits' pure abiding-place;
Tho' far remov'd from mortal eyes,
Faith views them in celestial skies.

There contemplates in realms above,
The seraph forms of those we love;
All bright, all beautiful, all pure,
From age to age they shall endure.

Behold the joy that reigns around—
Whence comes that soft, harmonious sound?
The Hymn of ransom'd Bliss they sing,
To Christ their Saviour, God, and King.

With loud Hosannas they adore
The love of Jesus evermore;
O may their Joy reflect on Earth,
To cheer us with celestial mirth.

Come, let us watch and daily toil,
To trim our Lamps with heav'nly oil:
Be ready thus to meet our Lord,
And chant his Love with one accord.

Thus all unite on Earth, in Heav'n,
In songs of Glory to Christ giv'n;
Attune our Harps, our voices raise
With Hallelujah's blissful Praise.

ON CONTRIBUTING TO THE BIBLE SOCIETY.

Lord, accept my humble Mite,
   Offered with a heart sincere:
May it help to spread the light
   Of the Gospel, far and near.

May the Pearl beyond all price,
  Anxiously be sought by all :
Let its value each entice
  To attend their Saviour's call.

May the Bread be quickly found,
  Which upon the Water's cast ;
May the precious Seed take ground—
  Yield a Harvest rich at last.

May the Nations of the Earth
  So their Bible learn to prize,
That, attaining second Birth,
  They shall all to Glory rise.

Bless the Missionary Band
  With thy Holy Spirit's aid,
Prosper them in ev'ry land,
  Let their efforts be repaid.

Then shall "Peace on Earth" be found—
  Joy shall beam from ev'ry eye—
Voices singing all around,
  " Glory be to God on High."

LINES ADDRESSED TO A SISTER,
ON HER MARRIAGE.

Sister, accept the simple Verse
  That flows from Love's pure stream;
O! that in rhyme I could rehearse,
  The hope I fondly dream.

To say how much I love you, Dear,
  Words cannot fully tell;
Forgive me, then, the rising Tear,
  When wishing you Farewell.

Recall the many days and years
  That we've together spent:
Uniting both our hopes and fears,
  We lov'd and liv'd content.

But I'll not grieve that we must part,
  I know 'tis wrong of me,
Since you've bestow'd your hand and heart
  On one who doats on thee.

United, then, to him you love,
  By Hymen's sacred knot,
May ev'ry Blessing from above,
  Attend your future lot.

May many happy Years be thine,
  Unsullied by all care,
And may each Year thy virtue shine,
  Still brighter and more fair.

I have but one request to make—
  Forget not what I say—
For friendship's, and for love's pure sake,
  Remember me, I pray.

And when you're settled far from me,
  Let fond remembrance dwell,
On her who'll often think of thee,
  And daily wish you well.

May that sweet friendship still subsist
  Which oft has smooth'd our way,
Nor time nor change its pow'r resist,
  Nor ought abate its sway.

When here below thy days shall end,
  And thou thy course hast run,
May then thy Soul to Heav'n ascend,
  And dwell with God the Son.

That dear Redeemer, ever kind
  To those who on Him rest:
O! seek Him now, for then you'll find
  Yourself for ever blest.

Tho' far apart we here may dwell,
   God's holy will be done ;
In Heav'n, we need not bid farewell,
   For parting there, is none.

Meeting with all we love below,
   With those we hold so dear,
Enjoying Bliss that none can know,
   While they continue here.

May such, then, be thy blessed state,
   With God thy Heav'nly Friend;
May Happiness commence its date
   Where time shall have no end.

ODE TO DOMESTIC BLISS.

Domestic Bliss! Benignant Pow'r!
   Sent kindly from the realms above,
To cheer us in each trying hour,
   To sactify, exalt our Love.

Ah! let me own thy blissful reign,
   Peace then shall flourish in my breast :
Enliven'd by thy brilliant flame,
   I shall indeed be highly blest.

In unison with all my views
  Of all that I consider dear,
Domestic Bliss, 'tis thee I choose,
  While I have life, that life to cheer.

True, I enjoy all lively mirth,
  But yet I never sigh to roam :
Give me that Paradise on Earth,
  The peaceful Happiness of Home.

'Tis here I meet pure Friendship's smiles,
  The tender glance of Love I see :
While social pleasure time beguiles,
  These render Home thus dear to me.

Come, then, bright Seraph of the Skies,
  I ask a favour. Grant me this :—
While I have life, whate'er arise,
  Be ever mine, Domestic Bliss.

MY SUPREME WISH.

O! may my heart with love o'erflow—
My bosom with affection glow—
With all around me be sincere,
And to my friends be very dear.

To love and be lov'd I aspire,
By God and Them, my fond desire ;
To love and be lov'd is my aim,
The joy I seek, the wish I claim.
I know no joy compar'd to this,
The purest of all earthly Bliss ;
Almighty Source of Peace and Love,
Grant me this Blessing from above;
Then shall a calm pervade my breast,
Charming each anxious thought to rest,
Diffusing Bliss enjoy'd by those
Who on their Saviour's Love repose.

ODE TO FAITH, HOPE, AND LOVE.

Faith, Hope, and Love ! how angelic the Three !
Yet Thou, most divine Belov'd Charity !
Hope may support us, and Faith can sustain—
Love, only Love, o'er our Spirits shall reign.

Faith is a Beacon—'tis founded so firm
On that Rock of Ages, naught can o'erturn
Storms may burst o'er it—yet none shall prevail,
Till Faith's lost in sight; ah ! then it will fail.

Hope, to our Souls, is the Anchor, so bright,
That even sorrow it renders more light,
And gilds the future, in days of our ease,
With prospects fair, which assuredly please.

Love is a Spirit so perfect, so pure,
To endless ages still it shall endure;
Shining celestial, transcendent Above,
Love is our Heav'n, for our " God is Love."

"MY PEACE I GIVE UNTO YOU."

Ah! will my Jesus, give me Peace,
    Beyond whate're this world bestows?
Doubt not—God's favours never cease,
    To those who on His love repose.

Then, why my heart so troubled be?
    The Christian has no cause for fear,
Thy gracious Lord has purchas'd thee;
    Ah! listen to his accents clear.

" In my Father's House are Mansions,
    Far, far too bright for human view,
Room sufficient for all Nations;
    Yes, e'en a place prepar'd for you.

" Let not then your heart be troubled,
    Ah! neither let it be afraid,
If your soul, is truly humbled,
    The Comforter shall be your aid.

" Eye hath not seen, nor hath ear heard,
    Nor can the heart of man conceive,
The glories that I have prepared,
    For those whose Soul will me receive.

" My Peace I leave, My Peace I give,
    Not as the world, give I to you,
I came to die, that you might live,
    I go, to send my Spirit too."

Lord, accept the adoration
    Of heart and soul transfix'd with love,
For the gift of my salvation,
    For tranquil hope of Heav'n above.

What bliss, such gracious words inspire;
    How can I thankfully express,
My gratitude, my firm desire,
    To serve my God in righteousness?

May I devote myself to Thee,
  And spend the life that Thou hast giv'n,
In active praise for saving me,
  And giving me a place in Heav'n.

"PRAY WITHOUT CEASING."

Pray when first at Morn you rise,
  When at work, or when you rest;
Pray before you speak, or act,
  Be assur'd you'll then be blest.

Pray for pardon, when you err,
  Or for guidance, when you doubt,
Pray whene'er you're coming in,
  Likewise when you're going out.

Pray, that God may prosper you,
  Grant you wisdom from above,
Pray the Lord to dwell in you,
  Pray with joy—for God is Love.

THE CHRISTIAN WORKS FROM LOVE.

The Christian works, not to be saved,
He well knows, that is done,
Therefore he works from gratitude,
Because the victory's won.

Since Jesus purchas'd life for him,
With His own precious blood,
He thankfully devotes that life
In striving to do good.

He would not let his Faith be dead,
As it would be alone,
But joining it to Works, it lives,
And thus, is fully shown.

Since Jesus Christ, has promis'd him,
A Crown of Bliss above,
It is the Christian's ardent aim,
To prove his fervent Love.

A FILIAL TRIBUTE OF AFFECTION
TO THE MEMORY OF
A BELOVED MOTHER.

My Angel Mother! hast thou gone,
To join the Saints above?
Ah! yes, thy gentle spirit's fled,
To realms of endless love.

To Mansions far too bright, too fair,
For mortals to enjoy,
Which Jesus has prepared for us,
Pure bliss, without alloy.

Oh! were it not for Hope Divine,
What could assuage my grief?
In Heaven above, I feel thou art,
'Tis *this* brings me relief.

I think thy happy spirit reigns,
Around the path I tread;
I hope thou art an Angel now,
Then hover o'er my head.

I love to fancy thou art near,
Still watching me by day;
I love to think I'm pleasing Thee,
By seeking the right way.

God grant that I may strive to speak,
And act, as in thy sight,
Then shall we meet again in Heaven,
With mutual delight.

I know thou wert for Glory ripe,
Just like a shock of corn;
And Jesus took thee to Himself,
His kingdom to adorn.

How gently didst thou fall asleep,
When Jesus called thee home;
My Angel Mother I believe,
Thou wilt with Jesus come.

JUDGE NOT.

Ah! Christian, gently draw a Veil
O'er faults that love should hide,
Your pity let a Brother claim,
His frailties set aside.

Why censure thus the erring one?
What might have been your case?
Where would your wand'ring steps have gone,
But for redeeming grace?

Who made thy lot to differ? Say,
What hast thou not receiv'd?
Then glory not, can'st thou repay
The Lord, whom thou hast griev'd?

Ah! judge not, but be ever kind,
Nor hasten to condemn,
Perhaps the Saviour of mankind,
May see much good in them.

Reflect what you have left undone,
The follies of your Heart,
Then strive to lead the erring one,
To choose the better part.

Sweetly to dry affliction's tear,
To soothe the pang of woe;
To live to our blest Jesus near,
Ah! this is Heav'n below.

Fair Charity can never fail,
But with the Good abide;
Then, Christian, gently draw the Veil
O'er faults, that love should hide.

LOVE ONE ANOTHER.

Christ says, "A New Command I give,
  "Love one another, love and live,
"By the pure love, to others shown,
  "By *this* I'll prove who are my own."

What is the emblem of our faith?
  The Christian's special mark?
Ah! list to what our Saviour saith,
  "'Tis love's celestial spark."

"A New Command I give to you,
  "By *this*, shall all men know,
"If ye are Christians firm and true,
  "Your love will ever glow."

"Love one another, Greater love
  "Can no man show than mine,
"I even gave my life to prove,
  "How great was Love Divine."

Lord, may a brilliant ray from Thee,
  Illumine ev'ry Soul,
Celestial Love we then shall see,
  Extend from Pole to Pole.

Come, then, Lord Jesus, quickly come,
    And send thy Holy Dove,
To guide our happy Spirits home,
    To realms of Endless Love.

THE FRIST AND LAST MIRACLE.

The first of Wonders Jesus made,
    Turn'd Water into Wine,
While minist'ring to human aid,
    He prov'd himself Divine.

The last of Miracles Christ wrought,
    A welcome Feast He spread,
At His command, the Fish were caught,
    The Lord supplied the Bread.

The Fire, and Coals, and Fish all there,
    His bounty did combine,
Then for His Own to prove His care,
    Christ bid them, "Come and dine."

From first to last, how great! How good!
    Is Jesus, in His ways,
According us celestial food,
    To cheer our transient days.

What gratitude we owe to Thee,
  Reedemer, Lord, and King;
Ah! let our hearts and lives agree,
  Thy praise and love to sing.

Yes! Jesus still provides us Wine,
  'Tis His own precious blood,
And gives His body so divine,
  To be our Heav'nly food.

Then clothes us with a Robe of White,
  Fair, as the realms above,
Where Jesus Christ will be our light!
  Our Bliss! our Joy! our Love!!!

ODE ON TIME.

Ah, Time! that glides with noiseless feet,
  And steals away our years,
Who with thy swiftness can complete,
  Such magic it appears.

Tho' when array'd in sombre hue,
  We wish you far away,
Tedious and weary to our view,
  Appear each Night and Day.

Yet oft with bright fantastic form,
    Thou vanishest too soon,
E'er like the radiant breath of Morn,
    That fadeth e're 'tis Noon.

At thy sweet smile, hope seems so bright,
    And all things look so gay,
We fain would revel in thy light,
    Entreating thee to stay.

Yet evanescent as a wave,
    Whose course so rapid flows,
Not one short moment wilt thou save,
    Tho' life draw near its close.

Come, friends, since Time so transient be,
    Let us, each hour improve,
For then throughout eternity,
    All time shall melt in love.

THE ANGEL SPIRITS.

I love to trace, when the fond Spirit's flown,
Its brilliant course to heav'n's eternal Home,
When not permitted to remain on Earth,
What Bliss! to think of its celestial Birth,
To contemplate those Angel faces bright,
In glorious spheres of everlasting light.
The Old, the Young, the Rich and Poor all meet,
With joy unspeakable each other greet.
Ah! see these loved ones 'mid this bright array,
Shining resplendent in eternal day,
Their Bliss elysian, which no time can change,
No space can limit their seraphic range;
Who then can say, that those so very dear,
Are not permitted to be with us here?
Perhaps those light, aerial Spirits freed,
Are ministering Angels when we need,
Soothing our Souls, when sorrows deeply press
Cheering them with celestial Happiness.
Those Angel visits, tho' by us unseen,
May be the foretaste of that Joy Supreme,
To know that we shall share with them above,
The choisest Blessings of Redeeming Love.

www.ingramcontent.com/pod-product-compliance
Lightning Source LLC
Chambersburg PA
CBHW021432090426
42739CB00009B/1459

* 9 7 8 3 3 3 7 7 7 8 0 8 8 *